Coaches' Approach: It's How We Think!

Helping People Become Champions

Disclaimer

Dedication

In memory of my Loving Mother and Grandmother and to my children – there is nothing on the ground except dirt and poop – keep your heads up!

Table of Contents

Foreword

As we go through the battles of life

We ask for a chance that's fair

A chance to do or dare.

If we should win...let it be by the code:

FAITH and HONOR, held high.

If we should lose. We will stand by the road and wave as the winners pass by.

Day by day....we will get better and better!

Until we CAN'T be beat.... until we WONT be beat!!!!

Over the years, this poem has resonated with me like a song of my heart. Whether it is getting through a rough patch or enjoying a pretty normal day, these verses have kept me going. This is how I begin and end every practice, competition, group, and one-on-one coaching session. Sometimes out loud, but mostly to myself. It is the reminder that I am in service to others and to remain focused on them and their development. These lines represent being self-aware, self-confident, vulnerable, humble, courageous, and resilient. They have never failed to render inner-peace to me, and I think it is safe to say this is how I think!

Ever since coaching has become a subject of different books and articles, people have been fascinated by the mechanics of coaching. I have noticed that people are not only interested in athletes' performance now, but they are also interested in their coaches. To be fair, it is incredible how one person can help you find your destiny and set you on the path of success.

For people who have enjoyed success in their lives to some extent, coaching is the critical element, which guided them and their progress. The truth is everyone wants to be powerful and victorious, especially in professional spheres. At the very least, everyone dreams of creating a lasting impact in their lives and leaving an impression on others. I know many people who have mastered the art of coaching. This book is, therefore, a guide on coaching that discusses first-hand experiences as well as the practices used by some of the best coaches I have known.

As a professional coach, I have experienced that the mainstream dilemma of the day is to do, or die trying. Either you become a revolutionary, or you risk becoming immaterial in the world. It is my effort to help coaches and aspiring professionals tackle this wavering outlook on life and embrace the winds of change.

With the increasing emphasis on performance-based outcomes in business professions, the field of coaching has evolved and grown exponentially over a short span of time. Coaching is a process that allows people to deal with change and obstacles on a personal level. As people all over the world have become more aware of the power of coaching, the concept has evolved to cater to the needs of diverse mindsets. That said, you must also be aware that coaching is not teaching. In fact, it is about creating an environment for self-learning and professional growth; tool which are invaluable in every aspect of life.

This book has been written in four parts. The first part covers the fundamentals of coaching. The second part will take you on the journey of self-awareness. The third part will provide a first-hand experience from my life as a coach. And the final part provides you with a workbook that will help you understand 'how we think!' and indoctrinate you through action-oriented activities.

Let us set out together on the path of self-discovery, personal and professional growth as we lean into the mind of a coach.

Introduction

Have you ever been in a place where you felt you
were stuck and there was no way to move forward?
The kind of feeling that limits your ability to think
through, but you know that you have the ability to
transcend. The worst thing about being stuck is
that you know you are! Several years ago, I was
stuck! And, during that difficult phase of my life,
what I experienced from professional coaching was
that it works! I had built a hard shell around me to
prevent or reduce any further discomfort or
distress. I was aware of my state of being and had
to find a way to dig out and be resilient. Through
professional coaching, I learned to grow comfortable
and confident about the challenges I was
experiencing and accepting them as temporary, a
transient part of the journey through life. And,
change the focus to rebuilding my emotional
strength, in order to engage in open, honest, and
free flowing dialogue with positive energy, to
become unstuck.

The journey toward being unstuck is challenging,
but when I reflect on the whole process, my greatest
difficulty was in taking that last step. What do I
mean? On my journey, the first step was about the
recognition of experiencing personal and
professional challenges and wanting to excel

beyond them. I accepted those challenges and was willing to do the work. The first step in my journey was emblematic of driving along a mountain road and suddenly gripped by the rising fog. And, while driving into such elements, my driving instinct, brain sends message to foot, immediately slows the vehicle down, carefully assess the conditions, and <u>proceed</u>.

Having never driven on a mountain road in the fog, you do not have a driving instinct, an ability to assess those conditions, which will result in you coming to a full stop on the side of the road, flashing the hazard lights. In this case, you are unable to take the first step. In order to begin on this path, there is loads of information that you must know about: your overall driving experience, the ability to remain calm in arduous weather conditions, the vehicles performance characteristics, and the conditional of the road itself. To embark on a journey, previously unknown, you must be self-aware, possess the required tools, and willing to accept the external elements imposed upon you along the way.

Being a coach, I knew how to approach being stuck in a state of discontent. I knew how to gain access to qualified coaching services in my professional industry. As with the resonance of a bolt of lightning, my coach created an environment of trust, listened intently, de-cluttered my situation, and aided my emotional exploration and growth. This experience opened my mind to a world of new tools and methodologies that can be used to access and be uplifted toward achieving my coaching goals. My coach worked diligently, with an undertone, that reminded me of myself and how I care for and engage during my coaching sessions. That energy beneath each of our coaching sessions is comprised of empathy, selflessness, encouragement, and accountability.

The last step of my journey toward becoming unstuck was the greatest challenge, and was the most important part of the process. This final step is about believing that improved self-awareness, cognitive tools, and personal growth is an asset to you and be willing to transcend that mountain drive through the fog; today and everyday to come.

I wrote this book to share the value and importance of a professional coach. Coaches hold stations in every walk of life, with the intent to nurture all of the potential abilities into a harvest of repetition for the betterment of the individual. My request is that you receive the content with an open mind and if inspired, to learn more about coaching and how it may add value to your personal or professional environment.

Part 1 – Off-Season (Preparation)

The perception of coaching varies greatly, depending on the audience and the experiences with it. In many instances coaching has been viewed as a bag of gadgets to the untrained. They think that once they are used, they will lead the desired results. While this is partially true, you cannot borrow this concept for long-term coaching and results. Such gadgets or tools might help you meet short-term goals, but even the best ones will fail when it comes to transformational change on various levels.

The truth is, know it or not; the results of coaching is unseen and unheard. The discoveries come from within the coachee, as they reflect on the discussions from the coaching sessions.

Your coach is a person that guides you in a way that no one else can. You think highly of them for the spirit and awe they instill into you. Your coach did something that is valuable to you and to almost everyone. You choose them as your coach because of how they did it. They achieved their greatness in the same way you know you can achieve your greatness. In this way, your coach is just like you, and thus, inspires you to be a champion too. On some deep fundamental level of truth within you, you know your coach has done what you know you can do too. It is like reaching one's most true and most powerful state of being and living. It is the best you can make from the combination of talents, gifts, and uniqueness that is you.

So, what external element is at play influencing the people that develop into greatness out of this human potential? Why is one person further along this path than another? What is the determining factor? Is it money, luck, talent, intellect, strength, toughness, preparation, work? Before I answer these questions, I want you to first understand what coaching is. This is important to understand because it can help you understand how a coach can unlock our true potential to help us become champions.

The Definition of Coaching

The simplest definition of coaching is to tutor or to train someone. It is interesting that the actual definition of the word doesn't help us much when it comes to defining the concept of coaching. This is because tutoring or training can be done in many different ways. Some of these ways have nothing to do with coaching in reality. Coaching, as a matter of fact, touches some of the most significant issues of our existence, like self-identity, spirituality, aspirations, and core values. So, for anyone who is planning to become a coach or receive coaching, you must be prepared for dealing with these issues.

All of us know of this word and basically what it means. We all have used the word at some point in life as well. Moreover, we most likely had coaches at some point throughout primary and secondary school. What is not intuitive is that her has never been a champion of industry, sport, entertainment, or politics without a coach guiding and holding them accountable. Ask someone who has a long list of accomplishments, and invariably they will be able to name a coach that calibrated them to transcend their talent. Coaching is unique, and there is no substitute. Nothing can fill the gap if there is no coach. Be it education, skills training, leadership training, teamwork, mentorship, partnership, preparation, practice, persistence, resilience; nothing can replace coaching.

There are many relationships similar to those you may have with your coaches: parents, supervisors, mentors, and peers. But if someone proposed to you, "will you be my coach". At the very least, you'd have to ask, "For what? And what do you need coaching for?" If the person responds, "Because I want to improve on some idea such as working to become a professional writer or high school principal". You'd then realize the true meaning of the word coach, and most people at that point would decline the request.

To excel and become a champion, to achieve greatness and to be you-to-the-fullest, you need a coach. Regardless of the field in which you are working, you will always need a coach. They might change along the way, but working without one can mean sailing without a direction. Imagine setting out on a journey with nothing but a decision to reach a destination. Not only is that non-viable, but it also makes you stagnant. You need a primary focus, a realistic vision, and a reliable coach to take you where you dream of being.

Fortunately, coaches are clearly distinguishable. Not by their title or by the champions they helped create but by the unique way in which they think and act, and react. The greatest reward for a coach is to witness the moment of transformation in their coachee, a reminder that we have succeeded in a succession of excellence in the development of humankind. This alone, is the natural aspiration of the TRUE coach!

Part 11 – Pre-Season (Self-Reflection)

It is important to understand the nature of coaching when you set out on the path of working with a coach. Coaching has the flexibility to deal with a wide variety of personal and professional problems. Usually, in a coach and coachee relationship, both of them together determine the scope of coaching. The nature and scope of coaching are not limited to a specific issue or narrowly defined parameters. In fact, the idea is to help a person reach a higher level of performance, satisfaction, and learning. When people reach out to you to become their coach, they do not expect to achieve emotional healing comfort. They, specifically, want your help in achieving something that brings fulfillment and purpose in their lives.

There are a lot of coaching fundamentals that have become clichés over the years. So many phrases that coaches use feel redundant. People often groan and roll their eyes when they hear them. Phrases like 'we'll take things one step at a time,' 'what do you think you could have done better to do this task,' and 'you have to get the best out of yourself' are rolled out by coaches over and over again. These might have lost their meaning to you, but their true essence remains as valid as of day one. Despite being clichés, some things are still necessary to focus on. What a coach can do is ensure the same points are getting across in a more effective way.

Coaching typically means helping people attain optimum performance. However, this demands certain changes in attitude, behavior, and the overall outlook of things. Once you help your coachee unlearn what is irrelevant, only then can your coaching give these important clichés some substance.

The process of coaching begins with building awareness and responsibility. Awareness is basically having focused attention and clarity of a goal. Like our sensory abilities, awareness can also have infinite degrees. Coaching raises awareness and guides to sustaining it with the appropriate tools. It increases self-awareness in areas where it is most required. The objective is to build the ability and confidence of people to add valuable input to their work. This brings a natural change in their attitude behavior and performance. Subsequently, a coachee is able to build self-reliance, confidence, determination, and a higher level of responsibility.

Responsibility is incredibly important in pursuit of higher levels of performance. When people accept and take responsibility for their attitude, actions, and commitment, they are able to improve their performance substantially. When you demand and expect your coachee to be responsible and verbally delegate responsibilities; it makes them accountable for what they do and how they do it. This does not mean threatening consequences if they do not do it; in fact, the idea is to navigate them to feeling truly responsible.

A good coach can differentiate between a normal and imposed responsibility. There are two ways to delegate responsibility, but only one of them is effective. The first approach is telling the coachee that they lack essential communication skills and they must get training is an example of imposed responsibility. On the other hand, the same issue can be addressed by telling them that enhancing communication skills can be a great addition to their diverse abilities. And then asking them, "How can we work on that, do you have some suggestions and ideas?"

The second approach will make a coachee feel more responsible. They will look for ways to increase their communication skills and thus suggest some options to implement. What you did differently here is to provide them with a choice. This will make them feel responsible and motivated to bring about the change, which is needed.

In my personal experience, I have observed a lot of coaches that go by the first approach. They have an autocratic, dogmatic, and manipulative approach in coaching. It is essential for a coach to understand that offering people more choice is the secret to unlocking their undiscovered potentials. Your coachee should feel they have the flexibility to choose different options. They should neither be restricted in their ability to take actions nor should they be hesitant in exploring different options for progress.

As a coach, you should not communicate from a position of authority or lecture as an instructor. It should be an interactive relation where you both contribute in setting and implementing strategies. A coach and a coachee will agree upon the means of contact, i.e., face-to-face, over the phone, or via e-mail. Both individuals will choose the objective, focus, and action plan of strategies. Neither the coachee imposes this responsibility on the coach, nor does the coach keep them out of the process.

As a coach, the perspective of your coachee must also include their potential and their barriers. Most often, people cannot see themselves from a third-party perspective, and we are their reflection.

The job of a coach is to realize that each individual has a different background and different limitations. Factors that might be beneficial for one might not work out for someone else. Some of us are born into an environment with little barriers and lots of encouragement, while some are born into an environment with little encouragement and lots of barriers. The only thing, which is common among all, is that everyone needs a coach.

A coach tells people things that they aren't ready to hear and ask them to do things that are difficult. You cannot expect people to know it or even believe it, even when you are aware of their true potential. But with a clear plan and a smart approach, you can bring about this enlightenment in your coachees.

Some might find many coaches in their path all through their lives. Others, after being unaware of their potential for a long time, might eventually find a coach who cultivates their latent potential and launches them towards success. This means that the element of hardship is a part of the equation in the making of champions. It is easier to understand this when you observe the greatest champions in the world and what is common in their lives. You will notice that often it is those who have come the furthest and overcome the greatest odds, are the ones who become our world's legendary champions.

How Does Coaching Work?

Coaching is the art and science of change and transformation. Although there are as many models of coaching, as there are coaches, there are a few stages that sum up the process of coaching elaborately. I will explain each stage step-by-step to help you understand how it works:

Stage 1 – Self-Actualization and Awareness

Most people have a mental picture of their desired future. This can be regarded as a desire for self-actualization. This stage is typically about realizing your full potentials and being aware of your qualities and lacking. The role of a coach is to help coachees realize where they stand currently and what their destination is. This is like reaching from point A to point B. While this might sound considerably easy, in truth, it is not. From point A, where a person is currently at, to point B, the desired future destination, the path can be anything but straight. The path ahead seems like a lot of knots of impossibilities and challenges, which makes it impossible to see the destination. Unfortunately, we do not come into the world with a roadmap either. So, to navigate the path to our desired future, everyone needs a coach. Meeting a coach and starting a conversation helps people get clarity of their vision. This results in pulling them in the right direction towards their goal.

What keeps us from achieving our dreams is a lack of determination and honest feedback. Coaching helps us identify the challenges and then come up with contingency plans to overcome obstacles along the way. It is not surprising that a coach can even help people turn impossible into possible.

Stage 2 – Constructive Growth

Coaching is a process of laying out a clear path from point A to point B. People have varying degrees of awareness and different perspectives about the world, people, and themselves. Perception and awareness evolve over time as we learn new things, and our minds open up to new possibilities. A coach's job is to provide a coachee with the necessary tools and a guideline to take the next step ahead. Both of them study the possible challenges that come in the way of achieving a goal. Then together, they draft a plan to overcome these obstacles. As the awareness, consciousness, and competencies grow, their journey towards point B becomes easier and more fulfilling.

Stage 3 – Making Amends

When people set out on the path of their destination, they often come across a growth edge. The growth edge is a point or moment in your journey where you realize that things have not gone as you hoped them to proceed. In such moments, people need a coach to guide them through. Coaches help them understand what went wrong and how they can fix it. A coach's valuable insights and knowledge enable a transformational shift. A coach points out when you are taking too large steps, losing balance, and deviating from your plan. The coach then inspires a coachee to take a small leap towards big changes. Making amends helps people in implementing changes then and there to carry on the path of success and growth.

Stage 4 – Success in Reaching One's Best Self

The fourth and final stage is a big leap towards success and fulfillment. Once people have overcome obstacles with the help of a coach, the next step is to help them reach their best selves. This is especially a spectacular moment in a coachee's life, and even equally, especially for a coach. This development and success are different from external or professional achievement. Reaching one's best self is essentially personal and intrinsic. When people reach this milestone, they have finally succeeded in putting in their best effort in achieving their goal. The true essence of coaching is inside development. A transformational growth in mindset, wisdom, and experience help people in reaching their destination with flying colors.

The process of coaching is about bringing out the best in people. It is emblematic of a cistern; rainwater flowing within and purposed to nourish gardens readily sowed. The process of coaching is a journey, an exploration, as well as the cause and effect of togetherness, in becoming our best selves.

Part 111 – Regular Season (The Conversation)

Two coaches are attending an industry-coaching seminar, where they will be hosting a training session. Walking back from lunch, they crossed paths and proceeded to dialogue as they waited for the session to begin. They are sitting outside the conference hall, deeply engaged in a conversation.

Ms. Octavia Loren is in her mid 40s, has twelve years experience of working as an Executive Coach, Economics background and has a holistic style of coaching.

Mr. Everette Nance is in his mid-30s, a few years coaching experience, has an IT background, and has a coaching style based on standards and rules or democratic style.

"I think it is about making them feel that it's ok to not be ok sometimes!" Coach Loren states as she takes a sip of her coffee.

"No! Coaching isn't therapy. It is like product development. You work on it until you transform an individual into the reflection of the final product you have in mind," Coach Nance asserts with certainty.

"Do you mean instructing people to do what they might not be comfortable with?"

"Hardly! What I actually mean is facilitating decision making and goal setting with your input from them instead of dictating. But yes, it sometimes means guiding them to see what might not be visible to them otherwise. How would you coach an individual different?" Coach Nance asks inquisitively.

Coach Loren adjusts her glasses and folds her arms on the table as she reflects, "Well, I do agree that my goal is similar to yours, which is mostly goal setting and helping them make the right decisions. But I feel more like a parent in a coaching role. I like to push forward in a way that explains to the coachee that all events are related and that an individual is a sum of all their parts," she smiles as she notices the confused look on Coach Nance's face.

"I know this doesn't make sense to you just yet, let me finish. This means that in order for me to really help my coachees, I would have to pay attention to their complete growth. I would rather ask an individual to set an agenda and simply guide them along the way to feel them connected, balanced and full of purpose."

"Fair enough! Our styles might be different but both of us are targeting for the same goal more or less."

"Indeed!" Coach Loren affirms.

"A lot of people who have never had a professional coach, like some of my friends, they often ask me how does having a coach makes any difference," Coach Nance steals a quick glance at the wall clock, "It is still 20 minutes until the conference commences, would you mind sharing your opinion about that?"

"Of course! I'd really like to. I feel that it is the coaching part of parenting that gets lost in today's families and child development. And is the only part that can bring about the life corrections for those adults who are "stuck" and have extra obstacles to overcome. I think you would agree with me on this that we, all have been through the phase of life where we felt that life was only beating us down, and we had no clear direction to make our way out of the fog."

Coach Nance nods in agreement.

Coach Loren continues, "For the longest time, I thought that was it. That was the maximum I could benefit out of life. I had run out of ways to make things work. But then someone helped me see where I really belonged, what decisions I needed to make. So, I speak with a personal experience when I say this that a coach is a torchbearer who leads us towards our valued goal."

"You are completely on point and as a coach, I agree with every word you just said. But when an individual who never had a coach before..."

A sudden interruption occurred, a voice of a young woman echoed throughout the corridor, the coaches stared at each other with a puzzled look, the corridor suddenly appearing empty. The voice became clear and articulate, similarly addressing coaching topics.

Both of them look around to find the source of the sound. Neither are there any speakers in the room, nor could they make out the direction from which the voice is coming. It felt that the voice was coming straight from another dimension. There was something about the voice so clearly bewitching that both of them felt they were in a trance as they listened in absolute silence and wonder.

"I don't know where to begin. My thoughts seem muddled and I think no one would understand what exactly I want." She takes a deep breath and it seems it would take forever for her to continue. Both the coaches listen intently.

"I want to nail the right career position for myself, but I've no clue where I fit in. I know I have many skills, and for the first time in life I believe that I can take the plunge to start something new and bring the change my life needs." She continues.

"But do I want to keep working for this organization. It is the job opportunity that finally came my way after waiting for so long. But why do I have this uncertainty that I might not be prepared to move on to the next opportunity."

"Should I do an individual development plan and reassess my skills...don't' want to waste all of the learning that I've gathered."

"I don't know what direction to go in to, and afraid that I'm leaning toward staying in my position and role, only because that's all I have ever known...because it feels safe," the young woman sighs with exasperation and then continues, "I think this is where I'm struggling and I want to give it a real shot before I call it quits."

Maybe I can have a one-on-session with my boss about my development opportunities. Worst case, my boss will say no. And if we continue to disagree, then I would have to choose a career that works best for me. But is raising it to her attention, the right step to take?"

Coach Loren and Coach Nance both sat quietly staring into the space, unable to make any remark. It felt that a younger version of themselves had just spoken to them, taking them back to where their coaching journey first began. The air was thick with suspicion and disbelief.

Coach Nance, finally, breaks the ice; "I never thought I would ever make it out of that conundrum with the right answer when I was that young."

"Neither did I!" Coach Loren half smiles.

"But we did. I couldn't be more grateful to my coach for the way he guided me and showed me what I was capable of. Do you wonder how you could have done it differently if you were in place of your coach?" Coach Nance inquires.

"Oh, yeah, plenty of times!" Coach Loren shakes her head as she continues, "I have played that role over and over in my head, over the years. I think this has been an anchor for me to plan all my coaching conversations. I would ask my young self to evaluate herself in terms of meeting her personal needs. She would rate herself, at most, 4 or 5 out of 10." She pauses and traces the rim of her cup.

"I wouldn't have evaluated myself differently, I suppose." Coach Nance remarks.

"I think there are a few important questions that I would ask her to address:

- How are these issues related to her overall goals?
- What changes would make her happy?
- How does she want her coach to help?
- What changes in her current role can be valuable to her and can help build her confidence in her abilities?
- Is there something about the way her boss coaches her that is not getting through to her?

- What can be the best approach in her opinion to deal with this problem?
- Are there any drawbacks to the best approach?

These are some of the questions that would help me to design an action plan for her. I believe the best thing about this approach is that my young self would not only find a solution to her professional plight, but she would also have been able to bring an overall balance in her life with what she valued the most. How would you coach your younger-self?"

"Your approach makes complete sense. I think this would have got you through the first phase of coaching successfully. The only thing that would have been different with my approach is that I would engage my younger-self in a way that he would feel he is equally contributing to find the right solution. Let me elaborate."

"Be my guest!" she chips in.

Coach Nance smiles and continues, "I would start by restating my understanding of what my younger-self had said and then ask if I had understood it correctly. This would help him see my sincerity and trust me as a coach because I truly understand his challenges. Next I would ask a set of questions like you, one at a time taking the process slowly and not rushing to find a solution. A few key questions to gather important information are:

- How would he want the current situation to change?
- What personal values and strengths does he have to solve these issues?
- Here's what I observed in terms of why this is happening to him (stating specifics). How do these resonate for him?
- If he were to solve these issues would that help him in moving forward with his goals?
- Is there something about his current role that he can change to fix the problem?
- What options does he have for solving these issues?
- What are the new behaviors that he would practice?
- What would success look like when these actions are taken?

I would also take a quick feedback at the end of the conversation to find out how different he feels from when he first put forward his problem. I think there is almost no difference in the outcomes of the two approaches. Regardless of the difference in our styles, what is most common is the ability to connect and engage proactively with our coachee. What we both want is to grab their hand and help them realize that with a little understanding and the right effort, they can achieve their goal."

"I couldn't agree more with you. Coaching conversations are about being clear, compassionate, and curious. Our goal is to find a solution for a coachee's set of challenges while seeking their confirmation and committing to assisting in their growth."

"I think it's about time now!"

Both the coaches gather their papers and coffee cups, and stood up from the comfortable lounge chairs. They exchange an inquisitive look, before they walked confidently through the crowded corridor leading into the conference hall.

Part IV – Post-Season
(The Workbook)

Coaches Approach: The Workbook

The following activities are designed to provide deep insight to the person that is willing to accept the outcomes. I have used these to further develop my self-awareness and that of my coaches over the years. Remember: You are the only one with the answers, and with those answers, an ability to implement them. I wish you clarity and peace during the exploration toward becoming: an improved self! Welcome to coaching!

Pre-work:

Before starting your first coaching session, please take some time to self-reflect using the following questions. Please write-out your responses.

1. What brought you to coaching?
2. Why now?
3. What are the personal / professional goals that coaching can support your journey?
4. Have you prepared your mind to be challenged with the encounter of your true inner-self?
5. What is that thing you must accomplish in your lifetime, from this day forward?
   [Year 1; Year 3; Year 5; Year 10]

Exercise #1

(THE CORE VALUES) – "Who Am I"

The Core Values exercise is centered on You! Take out some personal time to think about what values are important to you. The list of values below should be used as a starting point, an illustration of the tools that are used as you encounter life and interact daily.

First review the entire list of Core Values, then select the top 25 that resonate with you. Step away from the exercise for several days, and then reduce the Core Values further to the top 10 that are most important to you.

Now, with you top 10 Core Values, please take some time to self-reflect using the following questions. Please write-out your responses from the perspective of a third-person.

1. How would you summarize your Core Values, as a character in your favorite book, movie, or TV show?
2. If you are familiar with this character, what role did they play and how did their peers receive them?
3. Can you explain the Core Values and how they are reflective of the person in you?
4. Are you living and being these Core Values?

Exercise #2

(THE WHEEL OF LIFE) – "A Balanced Life"

The Wheel of Life is an exercise and tool for helping to identify those core values and priorities in your life. In coaching, the wheel of life is used to establish the foundation of the individual and baseline for goal setting.

Take your time doing this, I would recommend 15 minutes or so. Put yourself in a place with no distractions and reflect on your life as a whole. And be completely honest with yourself. This is just the beginning.

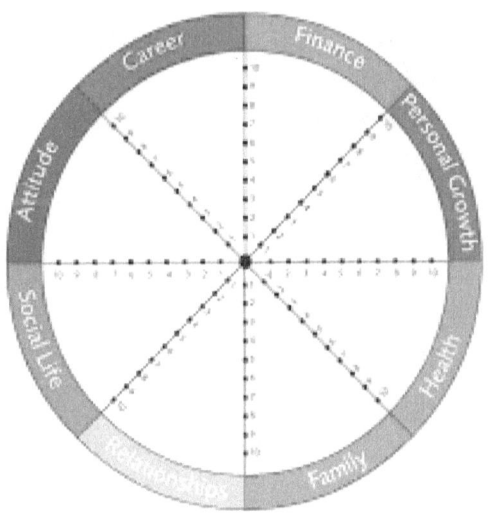

Scoring:

- If you have scores of 8 to 10 for any of the categories; you place a high value in this particular area.

- If you have scores of 5 to 7 for any of the categories, you place moderate value in this particular area.

- If you have scores of 0 to 4 for any of the categories, you place low value in this particular area.

Take a moment to appreciate your Wheel of Life. What does it look like? Are there any surprises to you? Are there areas that you would like to place greater value in?

Exercise #3

BECOMING A CHAMPION "IT'S HOW WE THINK...ABOUT OURSELVES"

After completing the previous exercises, allow several weeks to past before completing this exercise. The purpose is to create a statement about you using the information below. You do not have to use complete sentences; bullets points are best to convey your innermost thoughts. Accept the challenge to endure the obstacles and become a champion of personal development and growth.

1. **Self-Awareness – I AM...!**

2. **Self-Reflection – I KNOW WHY...!**

3. **Self-Integrity – I VALUE...!**

4. **Self-Acceptance – I WILL...!**